SO MANY QUESTIONS about...
RAINFORESTS

Sally Spray and Mark Ruffle

First published in Great Britain in 2022 by Wayland
© Hodder and Stoughton Limited, 2022

HB ISBN: 978 1 5263 1777 3
PB ISBN: 978 1 5263 1778 0

Editor: Paul Rockett
Design and illustration: Mark Ruffle
www.rufflebrothers.com

FSC
www.fsc.org
MIX
Paper from
responsible sources
FSC® C104740

Printed in Dubai

Wayland
An imprint of Hodder Children's Group
Part of Hodder & Stoughton
Carmelite House
50 Victoria Embankment
London EC4Y 0DZ

An Hachette UK Company
www.hachette.co.uk
www.hachettechildrens.co.uk

Have you ever thought about rainforests? Think of all the questions you could ask ...

I have lots of questions!

I can help. Let's take one question at a time and see what we can find out ...

What are rainforests?

Rainforests are some of the largest forests in the world. They get a lot of rainfall, which is why they're called rainforests!

In tropical rainforests it's always humid and hot. They can get over 2 m of rainfall per year.

Plants release water through their leaves and stems through a process called **transpiration**. It's a bit like the plants are sweating in the heat.

There are so many trees that it can take a raindrop up to 10 minutes to fall from the canopy to the ground.

When the Sun heats water the water evaporates, rising to form clouds over the rainforest. Some clouds drop rain on the forest again; other clouds travel across the planet to release their raindrops elsewhere.

Think about ... why rainforests are so important.

Rainforest are really important for the planet. It's thought that they store over half of the world's rainwater. We need them to keep creating clouds and rainfall for the whole planet.

O

Rainforests are home to over half of the world's plant species. Plants absorb a gas called carbon dioxide (CO_2) and release oxygen (O), during a process called **photosynthesis**. Rainforest trees lock up carbon in their trunks, helping to control climate change.

CO_2

And, it's my home ...

Rainforests cover about 6 per cent of Earth's surface. Astonishingly, half of all known animals and plants live there – that's 30 million species!

Would you like to explore a rainforest?
What would you take with you?
What would you like to look for?

How would you travel through the rainforest?
What would you want to avoid?
How will you cope with the rain?

Where are rainforests?

There are rainforests all over the world. Most are found near the equator, the invisible line that runs around the widest part of our planet. It's always hot there.

Tropical rainforest

Temperate rainforest

The largest is the **Amazon rainforest**. It stretches across most of the width of South America through eight different countries: Brazil, Bolivia, Peru, Ecuador, Colombia, Venezuela, Guyana, Suriname and also French Guiana (a territory of France).

Equator

Amazon

My family live in the forests of Central and South America.

There are two kinds of rainforest: the **tropical** and the **temperate**.

Tropical rainforests are always hot and humid. They have more species of animal and plant, and more constant rainfall than temperate rainforests.

Think about ...forests that you know.

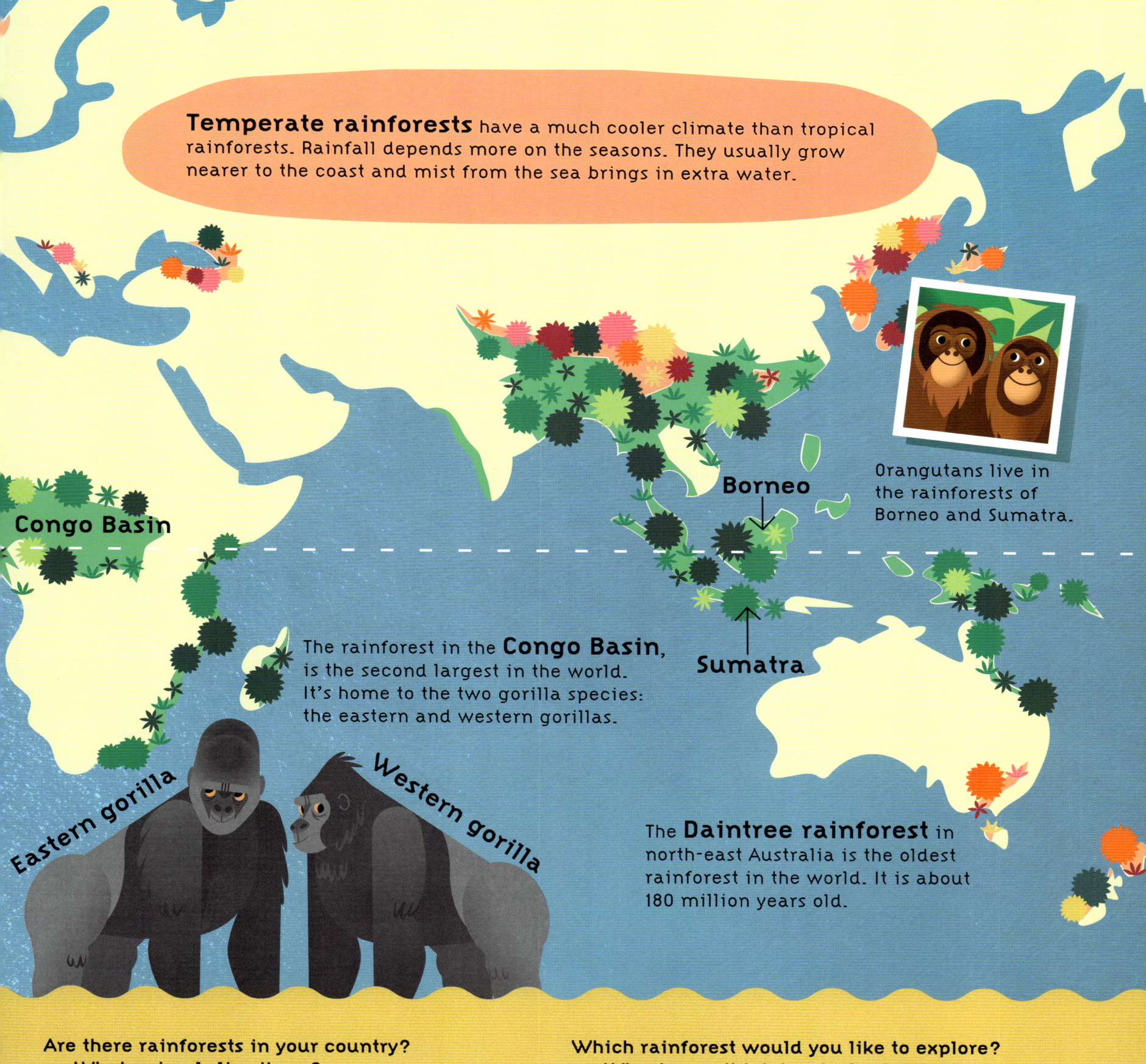

Temperate rainforests have a much cooler climate than tropical rainforests. Rainfall depends more on the seasons. They usually grow nearer to the coast and mist from the sea brings in extra water.

Orangutans live in the rainforests of Borneo and Sumatra.

Borneo

Congo Basin

Sumatra

The rainforest in the **Congo Basin**, is the second largest in the world. It's home to the two gorilla species: the eastern and western gorillas.

Eastern gorilla

Western gorilla

The **Daintree rainforest** in north-east Australia is the oldest rainforest in the world. It is about 180 million years old.

Are there rainforests in your country?
What animals live there?
What types of tree grow there?

Which rainforest would you like to explore?
Why do you think tropical rainforests are found near the equator?

7

What do tropical rainforests look like?

Tropical rainforests look a bit like this ...

They have four layers or storeys, and each storey has a different story.

Understory

Forest floor

Above the forest floor is the **understory**, the sheltered part between the ground and the treetops. The smaller trees and bushes found here are useful hiding places for frogs and snakes. Beautiful blossoms provide food for butterflies and birds. Jaguars hunt here.

Let's start at the bottom with the **forest floor**. It's covered with fallen leaves and fruit, and it's damp from rainfall. Moulds and fungi thrive down there. Insects eat rotting leaves and, in turn, are food for other animals.

Think about ... the different animals and plants that live in each layer.

Emergent layer

And finally, the **emergent layer** where the tallest treetops poke up above the others, stretching up to reach the sunlight. Birds and bats live up here.

Canopy

Next is the **canopy**, formed by the treetops. It's packed with branches, leaves and plants, preventing sunlight from reaching the layers below. Insects, monkeys and birds can be found here, snacking on fruit from the trees.

> I hang around in the canopy.

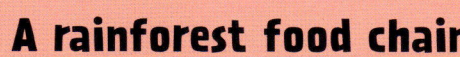

A rainforest food chain

Leaves → **Grasshopper** → **Paradise tanager** → **Emerald tree boa** → **Puma**

The warm, damp layers of the rainforest provide perfect conditions for thousands of plants, insects and animals. Each living thing is connected to others through food chains. Remove one element from the food chain and the animals higher up the chain will struggle to survive.

Which layer do you think people live in?
Which layer would be safest for sleeping?
Why does the sloth live in the canopy?

What noises would you hear in a rainforest?
What other animals could be included in the rainforest food chain?

What do we use from rainforests?

There are all sorts of products we use and eat every day that come from tropical rainforests.

People chop down rainforest trees to make furniture from **teak, mahogany** and **rosewood trees.**

Latex is collected from rubber trees and used to make gloves, tyres and other things.

We make hot drinks from **tea leaves, coffee beans** and **cocoa beans.** They all come from plants that grow in rainforests.

People weave baskets from **palm leaves.**

Think about ... foods that grow in the rainforest.

Did you know that a quarter of all medicines come from rainforest plants? **Cordoncillo** is used as an anaesthetic, **pusangade motelo** calms worries, and **quinine** treats malaria.

This **durian fruit** is super stinky, but tasty!

Fancy doing some baking? **Cane sugar, cinnamon, vanilla** and **chocolate** all come from plants which grow in tropical areas.

We can help people care for rainforests by buying Fairtrade and rainforest-friendly products. Our choices can make a difference.

Mmmm, look at all the rainforest fruit and nuts ... We've got **bananas, avocados, oranges, lychees, figs, mangoes, Brazil nuts, cashews** and even **pineapples**. You can also make clothes from the leaf fibres of the pineapple plant.

Read the labels on fresh food and packaged food at home. Which might have come from a rainforest?

What's your favourite rainforest fruit? What rainforest food would you like to try?

Which animals live in the rainforest?

There are all sorts of wonderful animals that live in rainforests across the world. Let's meet some of them ...

We're **squirrel monkeys!** We're expert climbers who live in large family groups in the canopy.

Hello, I'm a shy **agouti**. I love Brazil nuts! Sometimes, I bury them for later, forget where they are, and they grow into a tree.

I'm a **six-banded armadillo**. I sniff out insects and catch them with my long, sticky tongue. I've got armour and scales and can curl up into a ball.

I'm a shaggy **giant anteater**. I'm a close relation to the armadillo. I eat around 30,000 ants a day, sniffing them out with my handsome long nose. I carry my baby on my back to keep it safe.

Think about ... the different animals that live in rainforests.

We wee on our hands to cool down and use wee to our mark our territory.

I'm a **feathertail glider**. I can swoop between the trees, gliding on my skin 'wings', stretched between my front and back legs.

I'm a **three-toed sloth**. I stay very still … don't eat much … don't move much … sleep 18 hours a day. I'm sooooo slow that algae grows on my fur and helps to hide me from that hungry jaguar.

I'm a **jaguar**. You probably didn't see me because my beautiful fur keeps me hidden. It helps me sneak up on this lot for my lunch. Scientists say I eat 85 different animal species – I'd eat scientists as well if I could!

Which is your favourite rainforest animal? Which animal are you most afraid of?

How could you protect yourself from bigger animals? Which forests do these animals call home?

Are there rivers in rainforests?

Yes, including some of the longest rivers in the world. These include the Amazon river, which is 6,575 km long, the Congo river in Africa at 4,730 km and the Orinoco river at 2,250 km. Rainforest rivers are home to many amazing mammals, reptiles, amphibians and fish, like these here ...

The **green anaconda** can grow to be 9 m long. It's a constrictor and coils its body around its prey to suffocate it, before swallowing it whole.

The **black caiman** is a 5-m long super-predator. It's dark skin hides it from prey so it can swim towards them unseen.

Beware the **red-bellied piranhas**. They can be aggressive when water and food is low. But, most species of piranaha are vegetarians.

The biggest freshwater fish in the Amazon is the **pirarucu**. It eats other fish and has teeth on its tongue.

Think about ... life in rainforest rivers.

Poison dart frogs are tiny, ranging from 1.5–6 cm long. They're brightly coloured and deadly. The poison in their skin can kill big animals, even humans.

Flappy-nosed **proboscis monkeys** live in groups near the river.

Giant cane toads are around 15 cm long, though some have been spotted that are as long as 24 cm! They're very poisonous, even when they're tadpoles.

They love to dive-bomb and play.

They have webbed feet and hands to help them swim.

The **pink river dolphin** has pink skin that gets pinker when it's excited! It can swim the backstroke with its tummy up and its head under the water.

The **duck-billed platypus** can be found in Australian rainforests. It's an unusual mammal as it can lay eggs. It has soft brown fur, a beak like a duck, a tail like a beaver, cheek pouches like a hamster and webbed feet like an otter.

I like rivers, too! Sloths can swim much quicker than they can walk.

Why does a platypus look the way it does? Why do you think poison dart frogs are brightly coloured?

In which rainforests can you find these creatures? Which of these animals would you be happy to swim alongside?

Do people live in tropical rainforests?

Yes! There are around 50,000,000 people living in rainforests around the world. Many live in tribes that lead a traditional lifestyle, as their ancestors did. They understand the plants and animals and how to keep the rainforest safe.

The **Yanomani** live in South America. They live in circular, communal houses, called yanos, built in a clearing in the rainforest. Made from wood, leaves and vines, each yano can shelter as many as 400 people who live in family groups, each with their own place to cook and sleep.

Think about ... what it would be like to live in a rainforest.

As well as hunting animals for meat, the **Huli**, from Papua New Guinea, grow yams and manioc. They irrigate their crops by building water channels.

The **Penan** live in Borneo. Some are nomadic, making shelters of palm leaves as they travel and hunt. Many live in villages where they grow tapioca, bananas and rice. They don't keep animals as they believe that animals should live free until they are hunted.

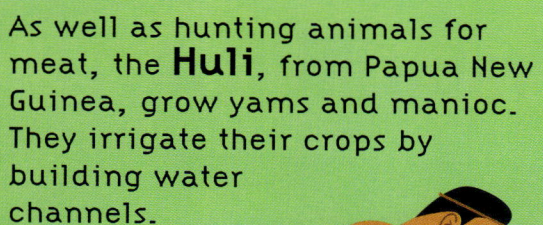

Rainforest peoples have many stories and beliefs linked to the wonderful forests where they live.

There are bird songs that bring good luck, and animal deaths that bring bad luck.

One myth warns of the dangers of swimming alone. If you do, a pink river dolphin might take you away to an underwater world called Encante, never to return.

If you want to see a rare Amazonian manatee, first be kind to a pink river dolphin, the guardian of the manatees.

Rainforest peoples are in danger from outsiders, who can take away their lands, cut down their trees, pollute their water supplies and bring in diseases.

Manatee

Pink river dolphin

What would be the sights, sounds and smells of a rainforest home? Who owns the rainforest?

What can we learn from rainforest tribes? What problems are rainforest tribes facing?

Which are the coolest plants the rainforests?

There are over 200,000 different species of plant to choose from! Without them, there would be no forest. There are giant flowers, plants that grow tasty fruit and even plants that kill!

One of my favourite plants grows in rainforests all over the world - it's the **banana plant**. There can be 240 bananas on each plant!

The most common tree in the Amazon rainforest is the **açai palm**: there are 5.2 billion of them. Açai berries are really good to eat.

Açai palm

Banana plant

The pretty **nerium oleander** is deadly. The stems, leaves and flowers are all highly toxic.

Think about ... why many different plants grow in rainforests.

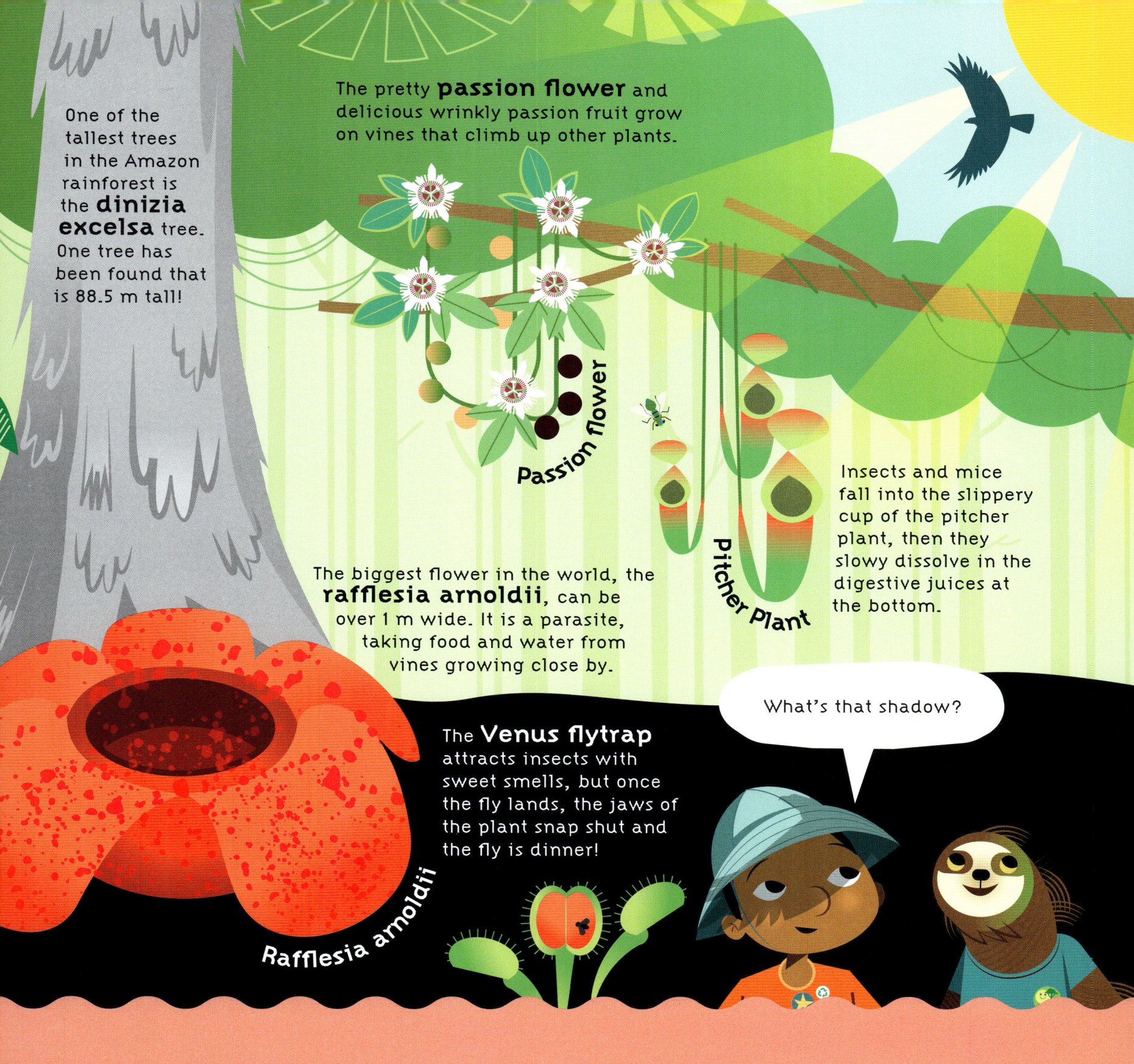

One of the tallest trees in the Amazon rainforest is the **dinizia excelsa** tree. One tree has been found that is 88.5 m tall!

The pretty **passion flower** and delicious wrinkly passion fruit grow on vines that climb up other plants.

Passion flower

The biggest flower in the world, the **rafflesia arnoldii**, can be over 1 m wide. It is a parasite, taking food and water from vines growing close by.

Insects and mice fall into the slippery cup of the pitcher plant, then they slowy dissolve in the digestive juices at the bottom.

Pitcher Plant

The **Venus flytrap** attracts insects with sweet smells, but once the fly lands, the jaws of the plant snap shut and the fly is dinner!

Rafflesia arnoldii

What's that shadow?

Why are some plants poisonous to animals? What other poisonous plants do you know?

Which plants are farmed in the rainforest? Which is your favourite plant and why?

Which birds live in rainforests?

Put me down!

About 3,800 different species of bird live in the world's rainforests. The one that just picked you up is a harpy eagle. It's huge, with a wing span of about 2 m. It hunts monkeys and sloths.

The **scarlet ibis** has long legs. It paddles in the shallows of rivers, looking for frogs and crustaceans to eat.

This is the colourful **toucan**. It loves to eat fruit and berries, smaller birds, eggs, insects and spiders.

Think about ... why rainforest birds have bright feathers.

Collared inca

Ruby-throated hummingbird

These are **hummingbirds!** Their beaks are perfectly shaped to suck nectar from flowers. Nectar gives them lots of energy for flying up, down, backwards, forwards and hovering to stay still.

Festive coquette

This bird looks a bit like a dinosaur ...

Reddish hermit

White-bellied woodstar

Casque →

← Wattle

The **cassowary** is 1.7 m tall. It can kick with its powerful legs, swim and jump to keep away from predators, but it can't fly.

The **potoo** is a master of disguise. It's nocturnal and keeps incredibly still during the day, camouflaged against a tree trunk.

Don't forget me! I'm a **scarlet macaw**. I eat fruits and seeds and I love to squawk!

How many species of hummingbird are there? Find out how birds' beaks suit the food they eat.

What's the biggest bird in the rainforest? What's the smallest?

Which rainforest bug has the most legs?

The giant millipede! It has up to a hundred legs and can be 30 cm long. Like most bugs in the rainforest, it lives in the damp rotting undergrowth of the forest floor. Here are some other rainforest bugs ...

The **Queen Alexandra's birdwing** is the largest butterfly in the world. It has a wingspan up to 28 cm.

The **giant millipede** is an arthropod. It has a segmented skeleton on the outside.

The **understorey** is alive with bright flashes of colour from the wings of many butterflies. They hunt for nectar in the bright flowers.

Some butterflies have long hindwings, like this **swallowtail**.

Think about ... why there are so many bugs in the rainforest.

Ants are the most common insect in the rainforest. If you weighed all of them together they would be heavier than all the other animals in the rainforest put together.

Bullet ants get their name because their sting feels like you've been shot!

Deep in South American rainforests live the biggest spiders in the world, the **Goliath bird-eating spiders**. They can weigh up to 170 g and have a leg span of 28 cm. They mostly eat mice, frogs, toads and lizards, but would eat a small bird if they got the chance!

Army ants work together to hunt and swarm over any tasty insects they find.

Which rainforests are home to the creatures on these pages? Why do rainforest butterflies need to be so colourful?

Which is your favourite rainforest bug? What other bugs live in rainforests?

Why are rainforests disappearing?

Rainforests are being cut down and destroyed by humans. In the last fifty years, half the world's rainforests have gone. Here's why ...

Trees are cleared for farming, to grow soya beans, palm oil and other crops.

People clear rainforests to build roads, mines and houses.

The need for electric power has meant that some governments in South America have built huge hydroelectric dams to generate electricity. The dams can cause areas of rainforest to flood.

Demand for wood to build homes and make furniture destroys rainforests.

People light forest fires to clear areas of forest, but the fires often get out of control.

People cut down huge numbers of trees to clear the land for cattle grazing.

Think about ... what the world would be like without rainforests.

The future of many animals is at risk with the loss of rainforest habitats.

Only 65,000 left

Toucan

Hyacinth macaw

Only 10,000 left

We need to save the rainforests.

The delicate balance of plants and animals is being destroyed in tropical rainforests. Really soon, some of us could become extinct and disappear forever ...

112,000 of us left

15,000 of us

3,000 **tapirs**

SAVE THE RAINFOREST

Orangutan

Jaguar

Why are rainforests so important for life on Earth? How would you protect rainforests?

Find out about an extinct rainforest species. Why did it die out?

What is the future for rainforests?

Rainforests face many threats. It's thought that 20 per cent of it has gone for good and an area the size of Great Britain is lost each year. More needs to be done to protect them. Here are a few ideas.

Wood source

Buy wood and furniture from companies that sell wood from sustainable forests.

Change demand

Reduce demand for beef and soya.

The money that can be made from farming leads some people to illegally burn down the forest to create more farmland.

Think about ... how to save rainforests.

Stop poaching

Lizards, snakes, parrots and monkeys are some of the animals people poach to sell as pets.

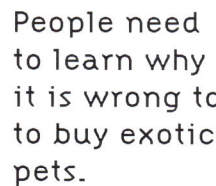

People need to learn why it is wrong to to buy exotic pets.

The skins of reptiles, snakes and crocodiles might end up as bags.

Please don't buy them!

Deforestation

Stop destroying rainforests.

Unite to help

Everyone needs to help countries where rainforests grow, as they are important to all of us.

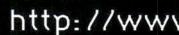
http://www

Support organisations that help protect rainforests.

Plant more trees

Keep replanting the forests.

It's over to you. The future of rainforests is in your hands. What can you do to protect rainforests for future generations?

Many more questions!

1. How many species of plant grow in the rainforest?

2. How does the agouti help new trees grow?

3. What does a millipede eat?

4. How many countries does the Amazon rainforest cover?

6. Can you remember the names of two rainforest butterflies?

7. What makes the Amazon river dolphin's skin turn pinker?

8. Where do mountain gorillas live?

9. Which rainforest creature grows algae on its fur?

10. If you visited a rainforest, what animal would you like to see?

Further information

Websites

www.rainforest-alliance.org

www.rainforestconcern.org/explore/forest-facts

www.natgeokids.com/uk/

Books

Cause, Effect and Chaos! In the Rainforest by Paul Mason (Wayland, 2018)

Expedition Diaries: Borneo Rainforest by Simon Chapman (Franklin Watts, 2018)

Follow the Food Chain: Who Ate the Butterfly? by Sarah Ridley (Franklin Watts, 2019)

Glossary

Algae – very simple plants

Amphibian – a cold-blooded animal that can live on land and in water

Anaesthetic – a drug used by doctors or vets to make a person or animal unable to feel pain

Arthropod – an animal without a backbone (an invertebrate), with its skeleton on the outside of its body

Camouflaged – hidden from view by matching the background or surroundings

Climate – the usual weather in a place

Climate change – changes in Earth's weather patterns, caused by greenhouse gases (carbon dioxide, methane, etc) becoming trapped in the atmosphere

Communal – a space shared by a group or community of people

Crustacean – an animal with a soft body divided into sections and a hard shell, such as a crab, lobster or woodlouse

Debt – money that has been borrowed and has to be paid back

Deforestation – the cutting down or burning of trees to clear an area of forest

Digestive juices – liquids produced by animals or plants to break down food

Endangered – a living thing that is at risk of dying out

Evaporate – change from a liquid to a gas

Extinct – died out – when there are no individuals of a species alive across the world

Fairtrade – the system where producers are paid fairly for what they have grown or produced

Food chain – words or illustrations showing how living things are linked together by who eats what

Fungus (fungi) – mushrooms, moulds, yeast and toadstools

Humid – air or weather that feels warm and a bit damp

Hydroelectric power – electric energy made from the movement of water over turbines

Irrigation – diverting water through pipes, channels or ditches to plants or crops

Latex – sticky white liquid made by the rubber tree and used by people to make natural rubber

Malaria – a serious illness causing fevers and shivering

Mammal – the large group of animals that gives birth to live young. Female mammals feed their young with milk

Manioc – a plant with white roots you can eat

Nectar – sugary liquid made inside flowers to attract insects for pollination

Nocturnal – animals, birds and fish that sleep during the day and are active at night

Nomadic – a way of life involving moving from place to place

Parasite – a living thing that lives on, or uses the energy from, another living thing

Photosynthesis – the way green plants turn carbon dioxide, water and sunlight into food energy

Poach – illegal hunting

Poisonous – something that could make you ill or die by drinking, eating or touching it

Predator – an animal that hunts prey for food

Prey – an animal that is hunted by others for food

Reptile – one of a large group of cold-blooded animals with scaly skin. Most lay eggs

Scavenge – to eat dead plants or animals

Segmented – divided into sections

Species – a kind of living thing. It can usually only breed or reproduce with other members of its species

Tapioca – a rice-like grain made from dried manioc root

Temperate rainforest – areas of forest, usually found along coasts, where the weather is mild but rainy

Territory – an area that one animal sees as its own, and defends against other animals

Transpiration – the way water evaporates from leaves, adding to water vapour in the air, and leading to more water being drawn up from the roots of the plant to all parts of the plant

Tribe – a group of people with the same beliefs, way of life and language, who live in the same area

Tropical – coming from the tropics, one of the hottest parts of the world close to the equator

Venom – poison from an animal or insect, injected through bites or stings

Wingspan – the measurement from the tip of one wing to the tip of the other

Yam – a plant with a large root which can be cooked and eaten

Game cards

You can play with the game cards in a number of ways:
Choose a rainforest animal card and get a friend to ask questions that you can answer with a yes or no,
e.g. Does it have wings? They can guess the rainforest card through a process of elimination.

Name Orangutan
Description
Orange fluff ball

Length 125 cm
Number of teeth 32
Legs 2
Lifespan 16,425 days

Name Proboscis monkey
Description
Long-nosed swimmer

Length 75 cm
Number of teeth 32
Legs 2
Lifespan 7,300 days

Name Jaguar
Description
Top predator

Length 150 cm
Number of teeth 30
Legs 4
Lifespan 5,475 days

Name Toucan
Description
Tropical bird

Length 65 cm
Number of teeth 0
Legs 2
Lifespan 9,490 days

Name Hyacinth macaw
Description
Beautiful bird

Length 100 cm
Number of teeth 0
Legs 2
Lifespan 18,250 days

Name Tapir
Description
Trunked snuffler

Length 117 cm
Number of teeth 44
Legs 4
Lifespan 10,950 days

Name Three-toed sloth
Description
Slow, slow, slow, zzzzz

Length 58 cm
Number of teeth 18
Legs 2
Lifespan 10,950 days

Name Army Ant (queen)
Description
Storming raider ant

Length 4 cm
Number of teeth 0
Legs 6
Lifespan 7,300 days

Name Mountain gorilla
Description
Gentle giant

Length 160 cm
Number of teeth 32
Legs 2
Lifespan 14,600 days

Name Bullet ant
(worker)
Description
Scorching stinger ant

Length 2.5 cm
Number of teeth 0
Legs 6
Lifespan 90 days

Name Giant millipede
Description
Forest-floor dweller

Length 35 cm
Number of teeth 0
Legs 100
Lifespan 3,650 days

Name Piranha
Description
Group hunter

Length 10 cm
Number of teeth 28
Legs 0
Lifespan 2,920 days

Name Armadillo
Description
It can swim!

Length 50 cm
Number of teeth 32
Legs 4
Lifespan 5,475 days

Name Goliath
bird-eating spider
Description As big as a
plate

Length 28 cm
Number of teeth 0
Legs 8
Lifespan 9,125 days

Name Cassowary
Description
Flightless bird

Length 190 cm
Number of teeth 0
Legs 2
Lifespan 18,250 days

Photograph or scan the cards, print them, cut them out and you can play the following games:
- Top Trumps
- Snap (you will need to print out two sets of cards)
- Lotto (you will need to print out two sets of cards)
- Matching pairs (you will need to print out two sets of cards).

Create your own rainforest cards to add to the pack!

Name
Queen Alexandra's birdwing
Description
Biggest butterfly

Length 38 cm
Number of teeth 0
Legs 6
Lifespan 90 days

Name Green anaconda
Description
Colossal constrictor

Length 901 cm
Number of teeth 100
Legs 0
Lifespan 3,650 days

Name Collared Inca
Description
Speedy hummingbird

Length 14 cm
Number of teeth 0
Legs 2
Lifespan 1,460 days

Name Scarlet macaw
Description
Bright, noisy parrot

Length 89 cm
Number of teeth 0
Legs 2
Lifespan 18,250 days

Name Potoo
Description
Nocturnal beauty

Length 58 cm
Number of teeth 0
Legs 2
Lifespan 1,825 days

Name
Duck-billed platypus
Description
Egg-laying mammal

Length 60 cm
Number of teeth 0
Legs 4
Lifespan 6,205 days

Name
Amazon river dolphin
Description
It's pink and cute!

Length 250 cm
Number of teeth 140
Legs 0
Lifespan 10,950 days

Name Scarlet ibis
Description
Elegant wader

Length 66 cm
Number of teeth 0
Legs 2
Lifespan 5,840 days

Name Harpy eagle
Description
Huge forest bird

Length 99 cm
Number of teeth 0
Legs 2
Lifespan 12,775 days

Name Squirrel Monkey
Description
Cheeky monkey

Length 68 cm
Number of teeth 36
Legs 4
Lifespan 7,300 days

Name Black caiman
Description
Awesome alligator

Length 421 cm
Number of teeth 76
Legs 4
Lifespan 14,600 days

Name Poison dart frog
Description
Colourful toxic frog

Length 6 cm
Number of teeth 0
Legs 4
Lifespan 2,190 days

Name Agouti
Description
Nutter for nuts

Length 50 cm
Number of teeth 20
Legs 4
Lifespan 7,300 days

Name
Feathertail squirrel
Description
Tiny gliding possum

Length 8 cm
Number of teeth 20
Legs 4
Lifespan 1,825 days

Name Giant anteater
Description
Insect-eater

Length 108 cm
Number of teeth 0
Legs 4
Lifespan 5,110 days

Index